MOVIE · POSTER · BOOK

Sex Symbols

DAVID MALCOLM

OCTOPUS BOOKS

Acknowledgements

The publishers wish to thank the following for supplying the photographs in this book:

Aquarius Film Agency 16 centre, 18 left, 28 centre, 44 right, 46 centre and right; BBC Hulton Picture Library 24 left and right; Camera Press 8 left and centre, (Roberta Booth) 27, (Harry Benson) 40 left, 40 centre, (Norman Parkinson) 42 left, (Terry O'Neill) 46 left, 46 centre and right, 47, 48 left; Countryside Colour Library 17; John Hillelson Agency Ltd (J.C.Sauer) 7, (Ed Sereny) 9, (Lorrieux) 39, 45; Kobal Collection 6, 8 right, 10 left and right, 11, 12 centre and right, 14 right, 15, 18 centre and right, 20, 21, 22, 23, 24 centre, 25, 26 left and right, 28 left and right, 29, 30, 31, 32, 34 centre, 35, 36, 37, 38, 40 right, 41, 42 centre and right, 43, 44 left and centre; National Film Archive, London 5; Rex Features 10 centre, 14 left and centre, 19, 33, 34 left and right; Transworld Feature Syndicate (UK) Ltd (Raul Vega) 13.

First published in 1985 by Octopus Books Limited
59 Grosvenor Street London W1

ISBN 0 7064 2371 2

First impression

Printed in Hong Kong

·CONTENTS·

·INTRODUCTION·

Sex symbols have been part of the movies ever since the screen's first vamp, Theda Bara (whose career was over by 1919!), enticed her innocent male victims to destruction with her flashing, kohl-rimmed eyes. And it is through the eye of the camera, as it captures and caresses these objects of our fantasies, that we can see how faces and bodies – no less than clothes – are subject to the dictates of fashion. From one decade to the next, legs grow longer and slimmer, as skirts do; busts become more generous with blouses following suit; the voluptuous gives way to the slim and elegant. Back and forth, across the decades, the pendulum swings.

Such shifts in physical style have, of course, always taken place. If we are more sensitive to them these days, it is because the camera has shown us how the bubbling vitality and warm prettiness of Clara Bow, for example, gave way to the cool irony and sculptured perfection of Marlene Dietrich; how the Mediterranean voluptuousness of Sophia Loren yielded to the slimline, all-American youthfulness of Brooke Shields.

Thus, film-makers – particularly Hollywood film-makers – are undoubtedly the great designers of human image. Year after year, these Diors and St Laurents of face and form unveil their latest 'collection' of models. Many of these are what might be called 'off-the-peg' performers – actors and actresses whose patterns of behaviour are only heightened versions of our own, and with whom we can all the more easily identify. But there have existed others – more stylised, more ethereal, more unapproachable – creatures of high fashion, as it were, with whom we identify only in our dreams. Psychologists tell us that we sleep in order to dream, not vice-versa; and it may well be that we go to the cinema for the same reason. Hollywood was, after all, dubbed 'The Dream Factory'.

Dreams, we are also assured, bear an intimate relation to sex. In consequence, the most potent of those to emerge from Hollywood's production line have been impossible sex objects, women who projected as much as they *were* projected, whom we could approach only in the dark, ambiguous diving chamber of the movie theatre. Over the years, some have faded and been replaced; but the most vivid and affecting have remained lodged in our collective memory. Carole Lombard and Marilyn Monroe may have died, they have not *dated*; Garbo's present anonymity cannot obscure the dazzling luminosity of her past beauty; Bardot, no matter how she might have aged, stays a kitten still. The cinema – a medium defined by Jean Cocteau as revealing death at work – is also that which has legitimised the age-old dream of eternal youth. And the pages which follow offer a portrait gallery of just a few of its more illustrious creatures, beings of a distant planet in which youth and beauty and silver-flecked sensuality have been preserved on film.

·URSULA ANDRESS·

·URSULA ANDRESS·

Born Berne, Switzerland, 19 March 1936

Ursula Andress's place in film history is a tenuous one, to put it mildly. She has never worked with a major director; never given a performance which could be described as more than adequate; and her future in the medium, as she soon approaches her fiftieth birthday, looks anything but rosy. Yet she will always be remembered for one role, that of the ambiguous heroine of the first of the James Bond thrillers, *Dr No* (1962). And, perhaps more to the point, she will always be remembered for one image: stepping out of the Caribbean surf, a harpoon gun clasped in her hand, like some busty, statuesque Venus in a creamy white, form-revealing bikini.

It may seem difficult nowadays, in the midst of the more permissive 80s, to understand the shock waves which that image sent through cinema auditoriums back in 1962 but, *Dr No*, it shouldn't be forgotten, was a *British* film – and, until that moment, the reputation of the British cinema had scarcely been one of flagrantly explicit, unashamed eroticism. What was also significant about the film, and the voluptuous Ursula's appearance in it, was that she seemed to herald the racy, sexy, carefree 60s, which were just around the corner. One might even claim that London began properly to 'swing' at the precise instant Andress emerged from the ocean. In a sense, such a close association with the period both furthered and restricted her career potential. She was cast, very much for her silky allure and overt sexuality, in a pair of characteristic 60s capers, *What's New, Pussycat?* (1965) and the dire Bond spoof *Casino Royale* (1967), the first of which, at least, enjoyed a huge box-office success. By the following decade, it was no longer enough in the movies simply to look stunning, alternately glacial and fiery; and Andress, who was less well endowed as an actress than as a physical presence, eventually found herself relegated to low-budget cheapies.

A few diverting roles enlivened her later output – as a glamorous countess in the World War I aviation movie *The Blue Max* (1966) and as one of a trio of chic bank thieves in *Perfect Friday* (1970) – but the films in which she since starred almost immediately vanished without trace. Her private life, too, has ceased to make headlines. During the filming of *Les Tribulations D'un Chinois En Chine* in 1965, she earned herself some (no doubt professionally valuable) free publicity from her affair with its leading man, the French idol Jean-Paul Belmondo, an affair which was at the origin of her divorce from the actor (and future director) John Derek. Of late, however, greater public interest has been focused on Derek's subsequent wife-cum-protegée, the luscious Bo.

The question of acting ability aside, it was Ursula Andress's misfortune to personify so vividly one particular type of beauty and to be associated with one particular period, the 60s. In consequence her reign as a sex symbol could not be other than it was: potent but ephemeral.

·BRIGITTE BARDOT·

· BRIGITTE BARDOT ·

Born **Paris, 28 September 1934**

It seems to help if sex symbols have surnames and Christian names beginning with the same letter: just as Marilyn Monroe was MM and Claudia Cardinale CC, so Brigitte Bardot has always been known as BB (it helps, too, that, as pronounced in French, this becomes a homophone for 'baby'). Not that she needed much assistance: nature herself was Bardot's talent scout. The daughter of a wealthy Parisian industrialist, she was a beauty at fifteen, when she posed for the cover of a leading woman's magazine, *Elle*. The Bardot of her subsequent heyday was already there, complete: the pouting, oh-so-French, and conveniently blonde child-woman image, for which the term 'sex kitten' was soon coined.

Three years later she met and married Roger Vadim, an aspiring young director who was to mould her public persona with films like *Et Dieu Créa La Femme* (*And God Created Woman*, 1957) and *Les Bijoutiers Du Clair De Lune* (*The Night Heaven Fell*, 1958), in which she made an indelible impression far beyond the borders of her native land. Unlike the reigning French sex goddess whom she was to topple from her pedestal, Martine Carol, BB was neither saucy nor coy. Sex came naturally to her, and she went just as naturally to it. There was nothing 'naughty' about the way she would casually display her breasts and bottom; Bardot was a lazy, intrinsically sensual creature whose natural habitat was the bed. Or beach. For she is still associated with the once sleepy little fishing-port of St. Tropez, for which she set an enduring fashion.

As an actress, Bardot's range seldom extended beyond sheer *gamine* charm and sex appeal, though she gave respectable performances in a handful of dramatic roles, notably H.-G. Clouzot's courtroom drama *La Vérité* (1960), Louis Malle's *Vie Privée* (1962), a semi-autobiographical account of a movie star driven to suicide, and Jean-Luc Godard's *Le Mépris* (*Contempt*, 1963). Despite the (no doubt ironic) title of Malle's film, there was little privacy in Bardot's offscreen life. Her frankly hedonistic existence with a cortège of pretty young boys in tow, her three stormy marriages (to Vadim, the actor Jacques Charrier, the multi-millionaire playboy-industrialist Gunther Sachs), not to mention a failed suicide attempt in 1960, made her the target of condemnation from various moral leagues around the world. Bardot was a classic 'bad example'. And it would be no exaggeration to claim that she changed our whole perception of what a sex symbol should be: her influence, conscious or unconscious, can be detected in such actresses as Nastassja Kinski, Goldie Hawn and Brooke Shields. She herself, though still photographed nude at an age when most women have celebrated too many birthdays to feel confident in their birthday suits, has retired absolutely from the screen, devoting herself to numerous causes involving animal welfare. Her type, however, will never be an endangered species.

·JACQUELINE BISSET·

· JACQUELINE BISSET ·

Born **Weybridge, Surrey, 13 September 1944**

Jacqueline Bisset is one of the quietest, least assertive of sex symbols, neither vibrantly carnal nor glacially slinky. Despite the vague confusion surrounding her name (often pronounced, mistakenly, in the French manner), there is nothing mysteriously cosmopolitan about her screen persona: she looks very much what she is, a nice English girl from the Home Counties. And extremely pretty, too, of course, if not quite 'the most beautiful actress of all time', as the magazine *Newsweek* voted her in 1977. Her English Rose beauty, however, is enhanced by an indefinable air of intelligence – she must be the least vulgar of erotic wish fulfilment figures. So that when, in a film like *The Deep* (1976), she spends most of its running time in a flimsy teeshirt with strategically placed damp patches clinging to her body, that beauty and that apparent intelligence combine with a superb figure to create a mildly indelible image of cinematic sexuality.

The intelligence is less evident in her selection of roles, as though Miss Bisset (the 'Miss' seems appropriate, somehow, in any reference to her) were more concerned to preserve an image of what used to be called 'class' instead of exploiting the potential of her star quality. Whereas Julie Christie, a not dissimilar icon, craftily expressed a very 60s fizz and effervescence, she has appeared in a ragbag of films, some of them good, most of them mediocre, none of them ideal vehicles for whatever she might have to offer. How many people, after all, can remember exactly what she got up to in *The Detective* (1968) or *The Life And Times Of Judge Roy Bean* (1972) or *Murder On The Orient Express* (1974)? In Francois Truffaut's *La Nuit Américaine* (*Day For Night*, 1972) she was charming if slightly distant; in *The Greek Tycoon* (1978) she played a thinly veiled Jacqueline Kennedy opposite Anthony Quinn's even less thinly veiled Onassis; and in *Rich And Famous* (1981), a personal project of hers directed by the veteran George Cukor, neither she nor Candice Bergen could erase from the memory Bette Davis and Miriam Hopkins in the film of which it was a remake, *Old Acquaintance*.

Yet, despite the fact that (except for the clinging teeshirt) Jacqueline Bisset's personal magnetism has been oddly muffled, there seems to be a quality in her which film-makers – and audiences – find irresistible. Perhaps it's precisely that ingrained 'class', in a period when Anglomania still reigns on Broadway and in Hollywood. Her appeal might be compared to that of Catherine Deneuve or the kind of blonde Hitchcock was so fond of using. No doubt, there lurks in every male spectator a sadistic craving to strip her of that demure facade, to corrupt the ineradicable 'niceness' of her personality. Whatever the reason, it would appear to be a fairly safe bet that she will continue to represent, with poise and composure, one of the facets of movie eroticism to which audiences in the 80s still respond, as they did in the 70s.

·CLARA BOW·

· CLARA BOW ·

Born **Brooklyn, New York City, 25 August 1905** Died **1965**

Few actresses have so vividly represented the period in which they flourished as did Clara Bow. She epitomised the 20s to such a degree that no history of the period can afford to exclude her. Dazzlingly pretty, with red bobbed hair, headlamp eyes and seductively pouting bee-sting lips, Bow was the flapper *par excellence* – a flighty jazz baby, game for anything. She would wink, flutter her eyelashes, raise herself up on tiptoe to kiss her boyfriend – in a word, she possessed 'It'. And what was 'It'? Nothing more than good old-fashioned sex appeal by another name. The term was coined (if one can seriously speak of anyone coining the word 'It') by the romantic novelist Elinor Glyn, who defined it as 'a strange magnetism which attracts both sexes . . . there must be a physical attraction but beauty is unnecessary'. As it happened, Bow was blessed with lashings of the 'unnecessary' ingredient, which, allied to her humour and quicksilvery volatility, attracted both sexes like iron filings. In a sense, she was an idealised version of the 'modern miss' whose type could be glimpsed every day of the week in the streets of New York: the only but crucial difference being that she was wittier, prettier and, indeed, 'Ittier'.

Bow was born into a wretchedly poverty-stricken environment from which she managed to escape by winning a beauty contest organised by a movie-fan magazine. Her prize included a walk-on role in a Hollywood film; and though real success and recognition came relatively late to her, from her mid-teens she was already a fixture on the industry's treadmill.

Not many of these early appearances have survived but, in 1927, she made an unforgettable impression as a flirtatious shopgirl setting her cap (or cloche hat) at her marriageable boss in *It*. If that modestly charming comedy has hardly aged, it is due almost exclusively to her unquenchable vitality. Bow retained her immense popularity for a few years longer by playing a series of variations on her most famous role. The only other of her films at all familiar to contemporary audiences is William Wellman's aviation drama *Wings* (1927), in which she co-starred with Charles 'Buddy' Rogers, Richard Arlen, and a youthful Gary Cooper who was one of Clara's extremely numerous lovers.

She made a handful of talkies, but the charm and charisma seemed sadly diminished: the 20s were over. Added to which, her reputation had been tarnished by a number of scandals. She was, for example, obliged to pay off the wife of a Texan physician who accused her of alienating her husband's affections. Then she received unwelcome publicity by incurring massive gambling debts in a Nevada casino. Finally, her career was all but brought to a standstill when her former secretary, Daisy de Voe, charged with blackmail, made noisily public her employer's dependence on drugs and gigolos.

Bow retired into sad seclusion, having married B-Western actor Rex Bell. When she died, in the 60s, she had been quite forgotten by the medium to which she had contributed so much simple but authentic pleasure.

·JOAN COLLINS·

·JOAN COLLINS·

Born London, 23 May 1933

Joan Collins is a survivor – of bad films, unhappy marriages (her husbands included actor Maxwell Reed and entertainer/composer Anthony Newley), personal affliction (her daughter suffered a near-fatal accident) and, ultimately, her own stale kit of seductive mannerisms. Almost uniquely among the cinema's sex symbols, she has reached her peak in full fiftyish maturity. As the ruthless, chronically scheming Alexis in the record-breaking TV soap opera 'Dynasty', she has become not only a household name but a campy, much-loved icon. Collins is also one of time's survivors. At the age of fifty-two, she can generate more behavioural excitement than all her 'Dynasty' co-performers put together; and if her own beauty is of a stylish, jet-setting conventionality, all *coiffed* hair and *haute couture* gowns, with not a *natural* bone in her body, this dark-haired beauty is still an infinitely more bracing presence than the blonde kewpie dolls and silver-templed sugar daddies by whom she is surrounded. So encouraging a model does she present to middle-aged women viewers that her beauty-hint guidebook sold in its millions.

Subtlety was never Collins' strongest card. Despite the two years spent studying at London's Royal Academy of Dramatic Art and her theatrical debut in Ibsen's 'A Doll's House', she knew instinctively that her most valuable assets were physical rather than histrionic. Her earliest roles, usually played in form-revealing sweaters and tight, bottom-hugging skirts, were as East End juvenile delinquents in a dreary cycle of 'realistic' British thrillers, for example, *Cosh Boy* and *Turn The Key Softly* (both 1953). An American period was scarcely more illustrious, especially as her rather endearing home-grown glamour was to be completely standardized according to the current Hollywood norm. In Howard Hawks' *Land Of The Pharaohs* (1954), she proved no more plausible an Egyptian than anyone else inveigled into that foolishly misconceived venture; and she seemed simply too British for the role of a Broadway showgirl at the centre of a sensational social-register murder case in Richard Fleischer's *The Girl In The Red Velvet Swing* (also 1954).

In fact, dreadful as the films were, it was only with her raunchy comeback appearances in *The Stud* (1978) and *The Bitch* (1979), based on her sister Jackie's lurid bestselling novels, that Joan Collins truly came into her own. And with her triumph as the malevolent Alexis, she can now fairly claim to have become a transatlantic institution. Vulgar she may be, crudely overt in her erotic posturings, but Collins is nevertheless a standard bearer for the type of old-fashioned glamour which was supposed to have gone out of style years ago. Nor can one deny her enduring loveliness, which allowed her to carry off the title role in a recent stage revival of 'The Last Of Mrs Cheyney' with such rakish self-confidence. We have not yet seen the last of Miss Collins.

·MARLENE DIETRICH·

·MARLENE DIETRICH·

Real Name **Maria Magdalene Dietrich**
Born **Berlin, 27 December 1901**

Jean Cocteau said of her name that it appropriately combined a caress (Marlene) with the sting of a whip (Dietrich). The English film critic, Gilbert Adair, compared her to some mythical creature, like a phoenix or a unicorn, and wondered whether, were the cinema not there to preserve the reality of her presence, future generations would believe that she had existed at all. With the possible exception of Greta Garbo, Dietrich was the medium's most sheerly *legendary* star, whose mystique and eroticism far exceeded the confines of her filmography; and it is worthy of note that, in the late 40s, when her daughter Maria gave birth to a son, Marlene's prestige was such that she managed to survive the dubiously camp (and, indeed, holiday-camp) compliment of 'the world's most glamorous grandmother'.

Much of the mystery in which she was shrouded, however, had been carefully fostered by herself. For many years, it was believed that her father was a cavalry lieutenant named Losch (he, it transpired, was only her stepfather); that the date of her birth was 1904; and that the film in which she appeared full-fledged (and exotically plumed) before an astonished world, Josef von Sternberg's *The Blue Angel* (1930), was her first. In fact, she had already acted in no fewer than seventeen German films of scant distinction (save for Pabst's *The Joyless Street*, in which, as an uncredited extra, she can be spotted in a scene with its star, Garbo). Nevertheless, it is *The Blue Angel*— with her immortal portrayal of Lola Lola, the nightclub slut— and the six subsequent films which she made with Sternberg that will preserve her memory as long as there are movies to screen and projectors to project them. In *Morocco* (1930) she sashayed into the Sahara as nonchalantly as though it were the beach at Monte-Carlo; in *Dishonored* (1931) she played a Mata Hari-like spy whose machinations brought her before a firing squad; and in *Shanghai Express* (1932) she was the equivocal heroine ('It took more than one man to change my name to Shanghai Lily'). Critics frequently compared the relationship of director and star with that of Svengali and Trilby or Pygmalion and Galatea, a comparison which Sternberg's wife took all too literally by suing Dietrich for alienating her husband's affections.

Though her box-office popularity gradually declined, Marlene continued to work regularly in the cinema, even managing to show off her fabulous legs as late as 1956 in *Around The World In Eighty Days*. And, at the end of her life, her glamour intact if by now slightly waxy, she made a fortune as a nightclub entertainer in London, Paris, New York and Las Vegas. Her appeal, still calculated to catch an audience collectively by the throat, was quite opposed to that of 'the girl next door'. No matter where one was born or how one lived, there was something alien and ethereal about her; and her lively sense of irony has ensured that her screen appearances will date as little as she herself appears to have done. No one ever lived next door to Marlene Dietrich.

·GRETA GARBO·

·GRETA GARBO·

Real Name **Greta Gustafsson**
Born **Stockholm, 18 September 1905**

Gar-bo: probably the two most famous, most mysterious syllables in the history of the cinema. As a woman, Greta Garbo is now more famous than any of the great historical or theatrical figures whom she incarnated in such heartstopping style – whether Queen Christina or Marie Walewska, Anna Christie or Marguerite Gautier (in *Camille*). And her legendary withdrawal from the screen, following the disaster of *Two-Faced Woman* in 1940, has enhanced the mystery a thousandfold. Today Garbo lives as a recluse, dividing her time between villas in Switzerland and on the Riviera and a New York apartment, occasionally sighted along Fifth Avenue, say, like some rare avian species, her dark glasses forbiddingly shuttered over her features. Notwithstanding four decades of rumours, she declined ever to make a comeback; and, in truth, she had no need to, for she has never really 'gone away'. Garbo is quite as much a star of her own private seclusion as she was of her public prominence.

Clarence Brown, who worked with her more often than any other Hollywood director, considered her the very prototype of stardom. Kenneth Tynan famously remarked that she appeared to a sober man the way other women appear to an alcoholically befuddled one. Yet the enigma of her appeal surpasses all verbal descriptions, however ingenious. The face must be *seen*. Hers was a beauty which did not rely exclusively on the cinema's great lighting cameramen to immortalise its lustre: unlike Dietrich, for example, a creature of the screen if ever there was, Garbo would have generated the same emotion on stage. Her performance in *Camille* (1937) was undisputably one of the most sublime in the cinema; and an enchanting light comedy like Lubitsch's *Ninotchka* (1939) demonstrated that she was equally at ease in less highly charged material.

Early footage of her in the Swedish comedy *Peter the Tramp* (1922) reveals a fairly pretty dumpling of a teenager, bearing absolutely no resemblance to the idealised ethereality of her Hollywood persona. The transformation was effected by one man, her discoverer, mentor and lover, the director Mauritz Stiller, who accompanied her to Hollywood but died (in 1928) before she had fully matured. And it was another director, Rouben Mamoulian, who perhaps understood most acutely the source of her attraction. When filming the last shot of *Queen Christina* in 1933, he commanded her to expunge every trace of emotion – one might almost say, of *meaning* – from her mask-like face, so that it be made a marbled *tabula rasa* on which every spectator could inscribe his own dreams and desires. Nothing has since happened to Garbo to flaw that perfect, pristine blankness – and her indestructible mystique finally leaves the writer, no less than the spectator, speechless.

·AVA GARDNER·

· AVA GARDNER ·

Born Smithfield, North Carolina, 24 January 1922

It's somehow reassuring to know that, though the child of poor tenant farmers, Ava Gardner was born with the elegant name by which she became famous. In spite of the starlet's treadmill to which she was condemned by MGM in the early 40s, the drama and diction classes, the calisthenics and make-up sessions, the core of her sex appeal lay in its authenticity. If she was, as the publicity for *The Barefoot Contessa* (1954) trumpeted, 'The Most Beautiful Animal in the World', why, she was born that way. Tall, statuesque and pantherine, she was one of the most ravishing creatures ever to grace a cinema screen; and even the fact that as an actress she could be stiff and inexpressive contributed to her sensuality, as it contrived to endow her come-hither eroticism with an untouchable, goddess-like quality. Sandwiched, in the roster of Hollywood sex symbols, between Rita Hayworth and Marilyn Monroe, Gardner was a dazzler who smouldered on long after making her K.O. effect.

She has always been cynically self-deflating where her career is concerned. When the columnist Rex Reed proposed a couple of titles of which she might be proud, she replied: 'Hell, baby, after twenty-five years in this business, if all you've got to show for it is *Mogambo* and *The Hucksters*, you might as well give up.' But she had more to show than that; and, in truth, Reed's titles were oddly chosen. By far her most memorable appearances were in two movies virtually conceived as frameworks for her beauty and luminosity: *Pandora And The Flying Dutchman* (1951), a campily supernatural melodrama in which, as an updated incarnation of the goddess of mischief, she helped lay James Mason's Dutchman to eternal rest, and was gorgeously enshrined in Jack Cardiff's pristine Technicolor; and *The Barefoot Contessa*, based partly on her own social whirl amid playboys and matadors. Curiously, she also played the half-breed Julie Laverne in George Sidney's 1951 Technicolored version of the Jerome Kern musical *Show Boat* and an Anglo-Indian in George Cukor's *Bhowani Junction* (1956); and served both Hemingway and Tennessee Williams well in adaptations of *The Snows Of Kilimanjaro* (1952), *The Sun Also Rises* (1957) and *The Night Of The Iguana* (a comeback appearance in 1964).

In the end, however, who remembers Ava Gardner's performances? It's as a tall, leggy, smokily glamorous presence that she remains lodged in the memory, and her tempestuous private life in no way detracted from the legend. Her three marriages – to Mickey Rooney, bandleader Artie Shaw and Frank Sinatra – were all equally publicized; and no self-respectingly glossy picture magazine of the 50s would dare hit the stands without a photograph of Gardner, accompanied by some personable male, making her progress through night-clubs in Paris, New York or Acapulco. Unlike many of her rivals, though, she judiciously and gracefully withdrew from these international playgrounds and now lives, quietly if not quite a recluse, in London.

·BETTY GRABLE·

· BETTY GRABLE ·

Real Name **Elizabeth Ruth Grable**
Born **St. Louis, Missouri, 18 December 1916** Died **1973**

If ever a woman was more sex symbol than actress or even star, it was Betty Grable. In a way, her whole career, spanning some seventy films, remained merely an adjunct to her personal appearance as immortalised in a celebrated pin-up poster that was to accompany thousands of GIs through World War II. Her legs were insured with Lloyds of London for over $200,000 – at a higher premium, then, than those of Fred Astaire or Marlene Dietrich. She was pert and brassy, a soubrette, and 'common' in both the snobbishly pejorative and populist senses. Pleasingly, she harboured few illusions as to the range of her gifts. 'As a dancer I couldn't outdance Ginger Rogers or Eleanor Powell. As a singer I'm no rival to Doris Day. As an actress I don't take myself seriously. I had a little bit of looks without being in the big beauty league. Maybe I had sincerity. And warmth. These qualities are essential.' For someone never exactly famous for her intellectual capacities, the above self-portrait comes surprisingly near the mark. 'Sincerity' is perhaps not the word, as that commodity was unable to survive long in the sentimental smog which permanently hovered over Hollywood; but what she may really have meant was sheer what-the-hell good nature.

From the evidence of her early career no one could have anticipated her subsequent superstardom. But, once into her stride in the early 40s, she scarcely put a foot wrong. Grable, in fact, epitomised the Twentieth Century-Fox musical, vulgar, garish and derivative, far more dependent on gaudy Techicolored sets and costumes than was the MGM variety, and far less dependent on real talent or invention. There were titles like *Down Argentine Way*, *Tin Pan Alley* (both 1940), *Moon Over Miami* (1941), *Springtime In The Rockies* (1942), *Coney Island*, *Sweet Rosie O'Grady* (1943), *Pin-Up Girl* (1944), *Diamond Horseshoe* and *The Dolly Sisters* (1945). Her leading men were John Payne, Don Ameche and Victor Mature, expressionless performers with blandly symmetrical good looks. (In real life a brief, youthful marriage to Jackie Coogan – famous child star of Chaplin's *The Kid* – was followed by a rather longer one to trumpeter Harry James.) It has been estimated that, in the whole history of the Fox musical, the studio's scenarists relied on three basic plotlines which they contrived to juggle together year after year – a case, really, of 'Dolly Mixtures' rather than 'Dolly Sisters'; yet, as populist entertainments marketing simple mass-produced pleasures, these films have retained a genuine charm.

Grable's fortunes declined precipitously in the 50s, a decade whose own roster of glamour girls – most famously, Marilyn Monroe – purveyed a less innocent brand of sexuality. According to the columnist Maurice Zolotow, she drily told Monroe: 'Honey, I've had it. It's your turn now.' Like the good trouper that she had always been, the blonde and bouncy Betty knew when and how to make her exit.

·JEAN HARLOW·

·JEAN HARLOW·

Real Name **Harlean Carpenter**
Born **Kansas City, Missouri, 3 March 1911** Died **1937**

There is a (probably apocryphal) tale of Margot Asquith visiting Hollywood in the 30s and meeting a number of stars. All went swimmingly until she encountered Jean Harlow, who persisted in pronouncing the 't' in 'Margot'. 'No, dear,' the exasperated Englishwoman finally snapped, 'the "t" is silent, as in "Harlow".' Apocryphal or not, such was Harlow's reputation at the time. She was blonde, brassy and phoney to the tips of, respectively, her platinum hair and her gaudily painted fingernails. To make matters worse, in 1932 she was the victim of cruel publicity when her husband, Paul Bern, an MGM producer, committed suicide on their wedding night, with rumours instantly circulating that his own sexual prowess had not been up to that of Hollywood's 'Blonde Bombshell'. Shortly afterwards, she embarked on a third short-lived marriage to cinematographer Hal Rosson.

Yet Harlow's notoriety proved in the end to have done her a grave injustice. Notwithstanding the hard, shiny, streamlined surface, the proletarian vulgarity and none too subtle innuendoes, she was possessed of real star quality and gradually demonstrated a considerable gift for comedy. The start of her career was inauspicious, to say the least. After eloping with a young Chicago businessman, she settled in Los Angeles, where she was almost immediately co-opted into the movie industry. Her first notable appearances were in comedy shorts for Hal Roach and Al Christie (most memorably, as a glamour queen in Laurel and Hardy's *Double Whoopee*). At that stage of her professional life, however, she was mocked by the critics, much as Jayne Mansield was to be thirty years later. It was only when she was cast opposite Clark Gable in *Red Dust* (1932), as a brazen but good-natured tramp, infinitely more entertaining a presence than her staidly patrician rival, Rosalind Russell, that she began to gain critical recognition. By the time *Bombshell* was released in 1933, her reputation as a sparkling light comedienne was so assured that she could afford to parody her own image. The film, in which she played a Hollywood sex symbol at the mercy of rapacious hangers-on and an insatiable agent, was one of the most amusing of the industry's satires on its own follies. Sex is fun, the message seemed to be, and it was a far more daring and subversive message in the 30s than it would be today. All the more absurd and tragic, then, that she should die in 1937 of cerebral edema, at the age of twenty-seven. Her last film, *Saratoga* (1939), completed and released after her death, was a hit.

Three decades later, two sensationalist film biopics of Jean Harlow's life appeared almost simultaneously, one starring Carroll Baker, the other Carol Lynley. Even if somehow combined, these two young actresses could not begin to recapture the witty sexuality of their much-lamented model.

·RITA HAYWORTH·

· RITA HAYWORTH ·

Real Name **Margarite Carmen Cansino**
Born **Brooklyn, New York City, 17 October 1918**

Rita Hayworth's filmography, stretching from 1935 to 1972, contains more than sixty titles, a half-score of them under her original professional name of Rita Cansino. Yet, to all intents and purposes, the only films of any real interest are those listed between *The Strawberry Blonde* (1941) and *The Lady From Shanghai* (1948). Of those preceding or following that period, the former are undistinguished and often indistinguishable B-movies, the latter a ragbag of comedies and melodramas from which most of the old allure has faded. So potent was the ravishing Rita's effect on 40s audiences, however, that she is still regarded as one of the most provocative of all Hollywood's 'Love Goddesses'. During World War II her pin-up portrait in *Life* was reproduced in its millions and adorned the walls of countless US Army barracks: it was even stencilled on the first atomic bomb to be exploded on Bikini atoll. She was an auburn-haired, brown-eyed, long-legged stunner, whose curvaceous figure looked as though it might have been poured into the slinky, satiny, backless gowns which set her off to such striking advantage. There was, at the same time, something refreshingly healthy and uncomplexed about her allure, as though she were a woman with a past which did not bother her one whit.

Notwithstanding her all-American appeal, Hayworth was the child of a well-known Spanish flamenco dancer, Eduardo Cansino. Discovered by a Fox executive while dancing in a Mexican border-town nightclub, she was signed up for a series of forgotten programmers. In fact, her career was stalling when she married Edward Judson, a businessman who applied his know-how to marketing his newly acquired wife, eventually winning her a long-term contract with Columbia. It was that studio which transformed her into a star with such personalised vehicles as the musical *Cover Girl* (1944), whose shiny Technicolor paid proper tribute to her magnificent mane of red hair; *Gilda* (1942), in which she sang (in a dubbed voice) 'Put The Blame On Mame, Boys', drawing off a pair of elbow-long black gloves with sultry aplomb; and *The Lady From Shanghai*, in which she played a predatory female gunned down by her co-star Orson Welles (the film's director and her then current husband) in a mesmerising set-piece inside a hall of mirrors.

As a star of newspapers and magazines, Hayworth remained a consistent headliner. It was as though the reading public could not learn enough about her love affairs (notably, with Victor Mature) and tempestous marriages (to Judson, Welles, Prince Aly Khan and big band singer Dick Haymes). In recent years, alas, the headlines have been of a different order. In 1977 a Californian court declared her 'unable or unwilling to accept responsibility for her treatment and a chronic alcoholic'. When last heard of, she had been confined to a New York hospital, tragically debilitated by Altsheimer's Disease.

·NASTASSJA KINSKI·

· NASTASSJA KINSKI ·

Real Name **Nastassja Nakszynski**
Born **Berlin, 1961**

Nastassja Kinski: her first name makes a near-rhyme with 'nostalgia', her second with 'kinky'; and it may be that the appeal of this exquisitely beautiful young woman lies somewhere between the nostalgic and the kinky. For she possesses the rare gift of appearing at the same time lascivious and demure, a kittenish 'child of nature' in the Bardot manner and a cool if meltable iceberg *à la* Ingrid Bergman, to whom she bears a remarkable physical resemblance. Kinski has become a star very rapidly, perhaps too rapidly. But though, as witness her Texan stripper in Wim Wenders' *Paris, Texas* (1984), she has an extraordinary knack for mimicking the most diverse of accents, she nevertheless brings to her American films a hauntingly subtle, almost intangible 'European' quality, an un-American reserve and vulnerability. In part, of course, our perception of her cannot fail to be conditioned by our knowledge of her background. She is the daughter of the actor Klaus Kinski, to whom – luckily for her – she bears no resemblance whatsoever; but since Nastassja has categorically refused to discuss her father in interviews, it's difficult to know precisely what their relationship was before their current estrangement. Another relationship, however, has been much publicized: that with her mentor, Roman Polanski, who cast her in her first starring role, as *Tess* in his tasteful, intermittently moving adaptation of Thomas Hardy's classic novel (1979). Though wholly un-English, Kinski gave a creditable performance, and an undercurrent of eroticism was created both by her similarity to the young Bergman and the audience's fore-knowledge of her liaison with the film's notoriously lecherous director.

She has continued to convey that hint of erotic mystery in films as disparate as Coppola's expensively stylised musical *One From The Heart* (1981), in which she played a tightrope walker out of Picasso's Blue Period; the strange paranoid thriller *Exposed* (1981), in which she *was* played, as on a cello, by Rudolf Nureyev; and Andrei Konchalovsky's *Maria's Lovers* (1984), as a small-town girl idolised by the Korean War-scarred John Heard. Yet it's remarkable that in those films where her sexuality is more overtly exploited, the enigma of her personality remains intact. In Paul Shrader's remake of the horror classic *Cat People* (1982), in which she was teamed with Malcolm McDowell, part of the updating process involved her playing several scenes in the nude. Such exposure in no way cheapened her image; somehow, somewhere, she succeeded in retaining the ultimate veil, and the image of her desirability was as deliciously frustrating as ever. This is a considerable asset for any actress; and Nastassja Kinski, also in *The Hotel New Hampshire* (1984), is undoubtedly the very brightest and most promising star of the 80s.

·GINA LOLLOBRIGIDA·

·GINA LOLLOBRIGIDA·

Born Subiaco, Italy, 4 July 1927

Gina Lollobrigida was essentially a figure of the 50s, not unlike Martine Carol in France. She was big and buxom, able to pout and swivel her hips with the best of them. Yet there was a standardized quality to her appeal, as though her undoubted sexuality was never more than an external trapping, as little related to her personality as a low décolletage or a pair of black fish-net stockings. Even if she did not strip on film, hers was the eroticism of a rather dated strip-tease act, the stripper herself remaining comically aloof from anything taking place further down her body. And when, by the late 50s, Sophia Loren's star was rising in the ascendant, Lollobrigida already struck one as an anachronistic throwback to a bygone era. Which might explain why the rivalry between those two stars was never of the good-natured variety.

'La Lollo', as she was affectionately known to the ubiquitous *paparazzi* (news photographers) who swarmed around her, was no actress; and, at least to start with, there was nothing in the films to which she was assigned requiring her to become one. Her first professional engagement was as a 'model' for the popular *fumetti* – romantic cartoon strips employing photographic stills instead of drawings. From these she graduated, via the requisite beauty contest prizes, to small roles in filmed operas, which resembled *fumetti* whose speech balloons were filled with arias. (Needless to say, she herself was dubbed.) After a couple of French excursions – the jolly period romp *Fanfan La Tulipe* and René Clair's *Les Belles De Nuit* (both 1952, both co-starring Gérard Philippe) – and a sensational Italian success, *Pane, Amore E Fantasia* (*Bread, Love And Dreams,* 1953), she was whisked off to Hollywood. For many years, however, her American movies were filmed in Europe, since she had become entangled in contractual wrangling with Howard Hughes. By then, in any case, the twin moons of her nemesis looked high, wide and handsome on the horizon. Loren was younger, earthier, sexier, and a better actress. So Lollobrigida found herself consigned to an incongruous joblot of cast-off roles: Sheba in King Vidor's turgid spectacular *Solomon And Sheba* (1959) or a flirtatious married lady in a limp adaptation of Feydeau's *Hotel Paradiso* (1966). Her sole remaining role of note was as the Fairy Godmother in Luigi Comencini's enchanting TV version of *Pinocchio.* The piquancy of her performance was much aided by the fact that Comencini mercilessly mocked her pretentions as a dramatic actress without her being quite aware of it.

Gina Lollobrigida is now, unbelievably, close to sixty years of age. She has retired from all involvement with the cinema, having assiduously made a second reputation for herself as a photographer. Her private life has been refreshingly free of scandal: she was for a number of years married – happily, it appears – to a Yugoslav doctor, Milko Skofic. By current standards, she perhaps cuts a dull and slightly ridiculous figure; and it's easy to forget what pneumatic delights were once conjured up by the very name 'Lollobrigida'.

·CAROLE LOMBARD·

· CAROLE LOMBARD ·

Real Name **Jane Alice Peters**
Born **Fort Wayne, Indiana, 6 October 1908** Died **1942**

It was Carole Lombard's special gift to possess not only oodles of sophistication but, in Sam Goldwyn's immortal phrase, 'warmth and charmth'. There was, about her presence on the screen, what one can only describe as a 'sheen'; and in view of the fact that she was perhaps the American cinema's most bewitching light comedienne, it's slightly unfair to categorize her merely as a sex symbol. She was one of the glories of the screwball comedy which flourished in Hollywood during the 30s and 40s, and no one who has seen her in Howard Hawks' *Twentieth Century* (1934), Gregory La Cava's *My Man Godfrey* (1936; she played opposite her then husband, William Powell), William Wellman's *Nothing Sacred* (1937) and Ernst Lubitsch's classic jet-black farce *To Be Or Not To Be* (1942) will have forgotten that potent fusion of droll spoilt-child petulance with an incomparably glamorous poise and self-assurance. Lombard was never crude or unsubtle, not even at the outset of her career, in the dozen silent slapstick shorts in which she was cast as foil to such broad comedians as Billy Bevan, Chester Conklin and Mack Swain. What she conveyed was flawless chic, humanised by the scatty glow of a personality which was not allowed to take itself too seriously. As one, alas, might well have predicted, she never won an Academy Award.

For an actress around whom the aura of star quality seemed to hover so visibly, Lombard was obliged to undergo a lengthy apprenticeship. Discovered at the age of twelve by the director Allan Dwan, she worked her way through Hollywood as other resourceful young women of the period worked their way through college. Apart from the knockabout two-reelers mentioned above, there were tiny roles in routine Westerns, comedies and gangster movies. But when cast opposite a performer of her own stature, such as the ferociously voluble John Barrymore in *Twentieth Century*, her personal magnetism was felt by every spectator. Lombard was always at her most memorable when a humorous complicity was established between her unique gifts for light comedy and those of some equally irresistible leading man.

These beguiling apparitions were brought to a sudden, tragic halt in 1942 when she was killed in an air crash while on a campaign to sell war bonds. Her fans were devastated, as was her second husband, Clark Gable, reputed to have been permanently scarred by her loss. Even the President, Franklin D. Roosevelt, made public his distress. In an unusual gesture of sympathy, he addressed this telegram to Gable: 'She brought great joy to all who knew her and to millions who knew her only as a great artist. She gave unselfishly of time and talent to serve her government in peace and war. She loved her country. She is and always will be a star, one we shall never forget nor cease to be grateful to.' Nor have we, for Carole Lombard was charisma incarnate.

·SOPHIA LOREN·

·SOPHIA LOREN·

Real Name **Sofia Scicolone**
Born **Rome, 20 September 1934**

Sophia Loren is the living – indeed, vibrant – proof that sheer earthy sex appeal functions in the cinema on quite another plane from acting ability. Despite a woefully undistinguished track record, both critically and commercially, from her early bit parts in Italian potboilers to her recent semi-retirement, Loren has been the recipient of both an Oscar and a Best Actress Award from the Cannes Festival. She has appeared in few films worthy of a place in cinema history – Vittorio de Sica's *La Ciociara* (*Two Women*, 1960), Anthony Mann's visually breathtaking *El Cid* (made the same year with Charlton Heston in the title role) and, if only because of its director's reputation, Chaplin's last, dispiritingly unfunny comedy, *A Countess From Hong Kong* (1967). Yet, like love itself, sex appeal conquers all.

What Loren represented was an Italian type of generously proportioned voluptuousness, dark, warm-blooded and close to the soil. Which meant that she proved most effective as a sex symbol in her earliest roles, where, clad in scanty, revealing and often sopping wet garments, she tended to be the object of some rustic passion. But she could also be feisty and humorously shrewish (as in her two Neapolitan farces with Marcello Mastroanni, *Yesterday, Today And Tomorrow*, 1963, and *Marriage Italian-Style*, 1964), poignantly maternal (as in *Two Women*) and coolly cosmopolitan (as in the glossy comedy-thriller *Arabesque*, 1966, with Gregory Peck). In fact, she was least 'simpatico' as a performer when taken up by Hollywood and 'glamorized' with pouting red-gloss lips and 'sexy' net stockings.

Sophia's popularity as a star has been greatly fuelled by her unusually admirable private image. She was 'discovered' when barely fifteen by the producer Carlo Ponti, who was then nearly three times her age, pint-sized, paunchy, balding and bespectacled. Their marriage, however, has endured to the present day as one of the cinema's happiest, although weathering more than its fair share of storms. As the union was not recognised by Italian law because of Ponti's Mexican divorce from his previous wife, the couple were charged with bigamy and, after years of frustrating negotiations, forced to switch nationalities and become French. Other problems included her series of miscarriages (before giving birth to a son, Carlo Ponti Jr), the theft in New York of $500,000-worth of her jewellery, and imprisonment in Italy for two weeks on a charge of income tax evasion. Recently, she played herself in a cloying TV biopic of her life, and it is a measure of the affection in which she continues to be held by the public that these embarrassments only increased sympathy for her. Whatever deeper passions she may arouse, Loren is without question the most *liked* of international sex symbols.

·JAYNE MANSFIELD·

·JAYNE MANSFIELD·

Real Name **Vera Jayne Palmer**
Born **Bryn Mawr, Pennsylvania, 13 April 1933** Died **1967**

Jayne Mansfield was essentially a photocopy, a pale Xeroxed facsimile of Marilyn Monroe. Considered from a certain angle, of course, she appeared to offer *more* than her predecessor – she was bigger and bustier, her cleavage yawned more dramatically, her buttocks protruded more provocatively, her lips pouted more seductively. And the publicity surrounding her was just as frenzied, but with a crucial difference: one never had the slightest suspicion that, as with Monroe, she might be harbouring some secret wish to back out of the limelight. Mansfield focused as tenaciously on the camera as it focused on her; she lived, breathed and, as it happened, died in the public eye. It almost seemed as though she made movies only to oil the public relations machinery, rather than vice-versa; and, in consequence, her filmography is one of the most consistently awful in cinema history. Apart from those films which no reasonably sane person is ever likely to have seen (such titles as *Dog Eat Dog, The Fat Spy, Las Vegas Hillbillies* and the posthumously released compilation work, *The Wild, Wild World Of Jayne Mansfield*), it mostly consists of cheap thrillers and near-pornographic melodramas. Only two films rise above the morass: *The Girl Can't Help It* (1956) – a timely spoof on rock 'n' roll stars – and *Will Success Spoil Rock Hunter?* (1957), a frenetic satire on television commercials, both directed by the former cartoonist Frank Tashlin, both making droll use of the CinemaScope format to encompass her (literally) most prominent assets.

Mansfield's ambition from childhood was to become a star – of what, precisely, seemed to have been of less consequence. And it was her good fortune to possess just those physical attributes most in demand in the 50s. Her acting ability was, to phrase it delicately, insecure; but, in compensation, she rapidly mastered the business of making her private life as screamingly public as possible. Who, living through that period, was unaware of her heart-shaped swimming pool, her shocking pink boudoir, her marriage to muscle man Mickey Hargitay, an exact male equivalent of herself, and, naturally, her vital statistics – never more vital than in her case?

But even Hollywood, for all its tawdry vulgarity, requires at least a semblance of talent – and it was soon clear that Mansield, unlike Monroe, was hardly less dizzy than the characters she played. So she became a joke, the point of which escaped her. The latter years of her professional life were spent in Europe where she connived, more or less willingly, at the crass exploitation of her parodic image. She died, horribly, in an automobile accident in 1967. By then, however, this sad figure could not have been more completely forgotten by Hollywood than if she had been an obscure octogenarian veteran of the silents.

·MARILYN MONROE·

·MARILYN MONROE·

Real Name **Norma Jean Baker (or Mortenson)**
Born **Los Angeles, 1 June 1926** Died **1962**

There have been other 'Marilyns' in showbiz history (Marilyn Maxwell, Marilyn Miller), and who knows how many women bear that name today in the UK or the USA? Yet, in the mythology of the twentieth century, those three syllables unerringly refer to one person, an almost supernaturally radiant blonde whose troubled and, in the end, tragic life story has aroused at least as much interest and curiosity as any of her screen appearances. The story is surely too well-known to need recounting at length. The wretchedly loveless childhood, as she was shuttled from orphanage to foster home. The notorious nude calendar pose which travelled around the world before returning to haunt its subject. The much-derided ambition to become a 'serious' actress, causing her to enrol at New York's prestigious Actors Studio. The unhappy marriages to a young aircraft factory worker, Jim Dougherty, to baseball idol Joe DiMaggio and to the dramatist Arthur Miller. The frequent bouts of depression and the infuriating tantrums on set. And, finally, her suicide from an overdose of barbiturates. Or rather, not 'finally'; for the Monroe industry has rolled on posthumously without any sign that it is about to call in the receivers. A compilation film was made of her career; Miller wrote an autobiographical account of their relationship in his play 'After The Fall'; and an unceasing wave of articles, books, memoirs, theories and revelations has inundated us since her death. In poor Marilyn's case, the 'P' in R.I.P. would seem to stand, not for 'Peace', but 'Publicity'.

The films remain, however, and will outlive the prurience: *Niagara*, *Gentlemen Prefer Blondes* (both 1953), *The Seven Year Itch*, *Bus Stop* (both 1955), *Some Like It Hot* (1959) and *The Misfits* (1961). No other actress in cinema history could be both so incandescent and down-to-earth, little-girl and all-woman, so shy and forthcoming, so vulnerable and sexy. As Joseph L. Mankiewicz (who directed her in a tiny but knockout cameo in *All About Eve*) remarked: 'When she stepped out in front of the camera, the camera liked her. In fact, the camera loved her.' Even when, as an actress, Monroe seemed stiff and unconvincing (as in many of her strictly dramatic roles), she was the focus of the audience's spellbound gaze. For though there were many feminine stars of the 50s whose vital statistics satisfied the obsession of the American male with outlandish mammary development, only Monroe could monopolise our attention with her tender and volatile features, her oddly innocent eyes and breathily pouting lips. It is possible that she was profoundly ill-at-ease enveloped by that fabulous body, that inside the statistically vital movie star there was a frightened little girl screaming to get out. Unfortunately for her – yet to the greater glory of film history – her screams were heard only when it was too late.

·BROOKE SHIELDS·

·BROOKE SHIELDS·

Born New York City, 31 May 1965

A curious phenomenon may be detected in the movies of the 70s and 80s: the advent of the nymphet. The American cinema has never been without a contingent of underage stars, from Jackie Coogan (Chaplin's 'Kid') to Shirley Temple, from Mickey Rooney to Judy Garland. What distinguishes the very latest brood of screen tots, however – Tatum O'Neal, Jodie Foster and Brooke Shields – is that they have all been cautiously exploited as sex objects. To be sure, the notion of sexuality here is one relating to cool verbal knowingness, less often to any overtly suggestive situation in the narrative. Nevertheless, Jodie Foster played a precocious floozie in Alan Parker's minipops musical *Bugsy Malone* and a child prostitute in Martin Scorsese's *Taxi Driver* (both 1976), Tatum O'Neal a cute, foul-mouthed bratlet in *Paper Moon* (1973) and *The Bad News Bears* (1976) and Brooke Shields a pre-pubescent whore in Louis Malle's affectionate evocation of a New Orleans brothel at the turn of the century, *Pretty Baby* (1978).

Though not the most talented or versatile of the trio, Shields is the one with the physical image most likely to help her through the ticklish switch to grown-up stardom. Even in *Pretty Baby* it was possible to anticipate the hearts she would break; and, with the passage of time, that beautiful cygnet has matured into an exquisite swan. Her sensuous, full-bloomed, dark haired beauty recalls that of Elizabeth Taylor at the same age, and her fashionably leggy physique (much in evidence in *The Blue Lagoon*, 1980) reminds one that she began her progress to fame by modelling for TV commercials.

Since her breakthrough in Malle's film, whose auction scene made her the most famous – or infamous – child in the Western hemisphere, Shields' career has hung fire; and the influence of her mother, said to be a relentless stage manager of her progress, may have been more harmful than effective. Yet, young as she is, she has already been tainted by scandal, with her much publicized suit against a photographer who marketed nude pin-up stills of her taken when she was only ten years old. Though she lost the case, the presiding judge referred to her as 'a hapless child victim of a contract to which two grasping adults bound her'. (As one has had cause to realize so regularly in Hollywood's history, however, such apparently adverse publicity may well further a star's career instead of obstructing it.)

The delicate green-apple charm of a child performer is, of course, an ephemeral quality, and Shields is now a poised young woman, frequently photographed on the arm of some personable Hollywood bachelor. Yet her example remains an important one. With her two arch-rivals, she undoubtedly breached an age-barrier in the perception of screen sexuality; and it would contradict everything we know of Hollywood's mental processes if, in the near future, her example were not emulated by other such diminutive sex symbols.

·ELIZABETH TAYLOR·

· ELIZABETH TAYLOR ·

Born **London, 27 February 1932**

Elizabeth Taylor, affectionately known as 'Liz', is perhaps the last great survivor of Hollywood's golden age. Coincidentally, she herself, as an actress, virtually grew up on-screen. She began her career as a ravishingly pretty young 'girl next door' in *Lassie, Come Home* (1943) and *National Velvet* (1944), scene-stealing from, respectively, a collie and a champion racehorse. As a teenager, winsome yet spunky, she graced *Life With Father* (1947) and *Little Women* (1949). The banns were called (along with those of her own first marriage, to the hotelier Conrad Hilton Jr) in *Father Of The Bride* (1949). It was in the 50s, however, that her almost supernatural beauty fully bloomed, and the title of one of her lesser-known efforts, *The Girl Who Had Everything* (1953), was perfectly, unashamedly, applicable to her dark, lustrous hair, deep violet eyes and fabled twin rows of eyelashes. As the Hollywood costumier Edith Head remarked, "When Elizabeth moved, she looked like sunlight moving over water." Then, ripening into maturity, she was prepared to play not only a couple of Tennessee Williams heroines but an expensive, sable-clad call girl in *Butterfield 8* (1960). Finally, when that sensuality degenerated into plump blowsiness, she was often able to capitalize on the ravages of time, offering one of her most memorable performances as a raddled, shrewish and desperately frustrated wife in *Who's Afraid Of Virginia Woolf?* (1966). There was therefore something quite poignant, even in her worst films, in our having to witness the gradual coarsening of a physical beauty with whose youth and freshness we had all been familiar.

As befits the last star of the old school, her much-publicized 'private' life attracted even greater attention than her strictly professional career. Public curiosity was inevitably aroused by her romantic involvements. After Hilton, and a doomed infatuation with Montgomery Clift, came marriages to British actor Michael Wilding, the flamboyant showman Mike Todd (later killed in an air crash), singer Eddie Fisher (thereby alienating the fans of his previous wife, Debbie Reynolds) and, most famously, Richard Burton, whom she met in 1963 while filming *Cleopatra*. Burton and Taylor starred in eleven films together, most of which were forgettable vehicles made specifically to exploit their enduring news value. In professional terms, then, neither career was enhanced by the relationship; but, in a world increasingly starved of good, old-fashioned glamour, however tawdry it might seem on occasion, they gave excellent value for money. And though she has been absent from the screen for several years, and was ridiculed for her overly ambitious stage appearances (in Lillian Hellman's 'The Little Foxes', and Coward's 'Private Lives' opposite Burton), it would be churlish to regard as a has-been an actress who has figured with such sheer style and sass in the iconography of contemporary cinema.

·LANA TURNER·

·LANA TURNER·

Real Name **Julia Jean Mildred Frances Turner**
Born **Wallace, Idaho, 8 February 1920**

Perhaps the most memorable moment of Lana Turner's career was that at which it was launched. Legend has it that, playing truant from school, she was perched on a stool in Schwab's Drugstore in Sunset Boulevard sipping a soda when she was spotted by an editor from *The Hollywood Reporter*, who recommended her to director Mervyn LeRoy for whom she made her debut in a bit part in *They Won't Forget* (1937). After which Schwab's, like the shrine of St. Bernadette at Lourdes, became a place of pilgrimage for similarly well-endowed young hopefuls (many of whom ended up by serving behind the counter). True or not, the story is characteristic of the tawdry fairy-tale quality of Turner's progress through Hollywood. Here was the archetypal movie sex symbol. She could act no better than certain glamorous secretaries can type, but she looked terrific in a tight sweater (which caused her to be dubbed 'The Sweater Girl') and, as one critic caustically remarked, 'changed her gowns more often than her expression.' What Hollywood achieved was to transform an attractive, busty teenager into a cliché of the brazen but alluring blonde, her features a permanent Max Factor mask.

In spite of the legend of her discovery, however, she was by no means instantly propelled into stardom. Lana Turner, in fact, rose slowly and laboriously from the ranks. She paid her dues in a cycle of forgotten little potboilers – or else was weirdly miscast as a prim English miss in *Dr. Jekyll And Mr Hyde* (1941), with Spencer Tracy in the dual title role. It was in *The Postman Always Rings Twice*, a 1946 adaptation of James M. Cain's thriller, that the pot finally boiled over. Though her performance was little more than adequate, and though she was again miscast – as the frustrated wife of a middle-aged cafe proprietor – Turner presented a vision of ethereal white glamour fully vindicating John Garfield's readiness to commit murder for her. Such vehicles, unfortunately, remained few and far between; and her sole Oscar nomination, for her performance in *Peyton Place* (1957), a hugely successful adaptation of Grace Metalious' crass but undeniably steamy bestseller, was a grotesquely generous one.

Of far greater interest to the public than her eternally sputtering career was her turbulent offscreen life. There were, for example, seven marriages, the most publicized of which were to bandleader Artie Shaw, playboy millionaire Bob Topping and erstwhile screen Tarzan Lex Barker. Even more sensational was an incident in 1958, when her teenage daughter Cheryl Crane fatally stabbed her mother's current companion, an underworld hoodlum named Johnny Stompanato. Cheryl was aquitted on the grounds of justifiable homicide; a number of torrid love letters were read out in court; and Miss Turner herself, playing the role of distressed mother to the hilt, suffered few adverse effects from the publicity attendant on the case.

· RAQUEL WELCH ·

· RAQUEL WELCH ·

Real Name **Raquel Tejada**
Born **Chicago, 5 September 1940**

There are stars of stage, of screen, of television, and there are stars of all three media. Raquel Welch is a star of publicity. She was publicized into celebrity, and it's almost exclusively through publicity that she has managed to retain her tenuous hold on fame. Though her filmography contains over thirty titles, it would require a fanatically devoted moviegoer to have seen even half of them. From a singularly unattractive list, one might just mention Richard Fleischer's droll science-fiction caper *The Fantastic Voyage* (1966), Richard Lester's pair of Dumas spoofs, *The Three* and *Four Musketeers* (1974 and 1975), and James Ivory's Fatty Arbuckle-inspired melodrama *The Wild Party* (also 1975). Then, simply for their notoriety, one could add *One Million Years B.C.* (1966) and the infamous screen adaptation of Gore Vidal's witty, cynical novel *Myra Breckinridge* (1970), directed – if that's an accurate term – by former pop singer (and now former moviemaker) Mike Sarne. And that's it.

Yet Raquel Welch has been, and still is, one of the best-known movie stars in the world. Certainly, she is not, in a physical sense, underprivileged. She is tall, voluptuously well-developed and genuinely beautiful in a conventional Hollywoodian style. (Beauty, they say, is only skin deep – and, on occasion, even shallower than that. According to the cosmetician George Masters, Welch is 'silicone from the knees up', and there have been persistent rumours of nose jobs, face jobs, etc). Her early years constituted a long period of gestation for the stardom she so assiduously courted: modelling, drama school, beauty contests and tiny walk-on roles. In 1963, however, she met Patrick Curtis, a promotions expert who immediately took her in hand. He marketed her as a product and, it cannot be denied, successfully. Though her film roles did not noticeably improve, the same cannot be said for the newspaper and magazine coverage which she received. In 1971, for example, when she and Curtis finally married, photographs of them in bed together were at once released to a presumably waiting world.

The problem was, as far as her career was concerned, that her incarnation of the 'eternal feminine', unapproachable because too unimaginably beautiful, was already out-of-date by the 70s, and Welch possesses neither the acting ability nor sheer force of personality to adjust her image. She recently enjoyed a genuine critical triumph as Lauren Bacall's replacement in the hit Broadway musical 'Woman Of The Year', but it is difficult to conceive how, at forty-five, a star so slavishly dependent on her looks and figure can hope to survive in the industry for very many years longer – though her recent glossy album of beauty hints was an international best-seller and Miss Welch herself an excellent advertisement for it.

·MAE WEST·

· MAE WEST ·

Born **Brooklyn, New York City, 17 August 1892** Died **1980**

If Hollywood actresses were to be categorized as boxers are, then Mae West would assuredly be entered as a heavyweight. In terms not only of sheer physical weight – always, in her case, an obscure statistic, given the bustles and corsets which beefed her up – but also of the erotic charge she so tirelessly emitted. To extend the analogy with prizefighting, it might be claimed that Mae always won her man with a K.O., never on points.

In her lascivious 30s comedies, *She Done Him Wrong* and *I'm No Angel* (both 1933), *Belle Of The Nineties* (1934) and *Klondike Annie* (1935), she presented an image of herself which seemed both ageless and unvarying. She was as opulent in form as the Madam of a brothel, with her thickly made-up features usually overshadowed by the brim of an enormous velveteen hat, on which perched a roll of ostrich feathers.

West's importance as a star lay in the fact that she introduced into the movies of the period the raunchy vaudeville humour with which her Broadway fans were already familiar. She was therefore a figure of fun but not of mockery, for the very excess of her personality allowed her simultaneously to exploit and parody the moth-eaten mannerisms of the man-eating vamp. Objectively, of course, she cut a preposterous figure – yet she was saved from ridicule on two counts. First, she was indeed, in an almost literal sense, ageless. During her bizarre comeback years, as the consenting object of campy cult adulation, she appeared exactly as in her heyday. In such movies as *Myra Breckinridge* (made when she was 78) and *Sextette* (when she was 85!) she was still capable of grinding out the sex appeal with great good humour. Which brings us to the second saving grace: she was that rare phenomenon, a witty sex symbol. A handful of her *bons mots* have entered the language: 'It's not the men in my life that count, it's the life in my men' and 'Keep a diary and it'll end up by keeping you' and, most celebrated of all, pronounced with the archest of leers, 'Come up and see me sometime!' She herself was the successful author of several Broadway plays, often unequivocal in title, such as 'Sex' and 'Drag'; wrote all her own screen dialogue and, in 1959, published an amusing autobiography, 'Goodness Had Nothing To Do With It'.

The vehicles in which West's talents were encased ranged from the very funny (*She Done Him Wrong*) via the atrociously tacky (*Myra Breckinridge*, a travesty of Gore Vidal's novel) to the simply unbelievable (*Sextette*). On stage and screen, her juicy innuendoes notoriously ran foul of obscenity laws (she was once jailed for ten days on Welfare Island); an inflatable emergency life jacket was named after her; and her lips were the model (presumably by proxy) for one of Salvador Dali's most endearing conceits, a red satin sofa. Her popularity, moreover, is now posthumously greater than perhaps it ever was during her lifetime. Both physically and in every other respect, Mae West was built to last.